AROUND THE WORLD IN EVERY VEHICLE

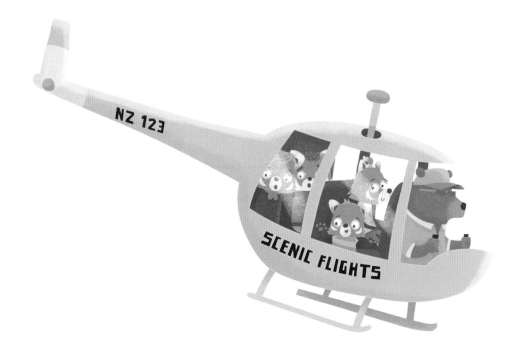

The little blue
camper van

Quarto is the authority on a wide range of topics.

Quarto educates, entertains and enriches the lives
our readers—enthusiasts and lovers of hands-on l

www.quartoknows.com

Author: Amber Stewart
Illustrator: Duncan Beedie
Consultant: Felicity Fitchard
Editor: Ellie Brough
Designer: Verity Clark

2018 © Quarto Publishing plc

First published in 2018 by QEB Publishing,
an imprint of The Quarto Group.
6 Orchard Road, Suite 100
Lake Forest, CA 92630
T: +1 949 380 7510
F: +1 949 380 7575
www,QuartoKnows.com

A CIP record for this book is available from the Library of Congress.

ISBN 978 1 68297 388 2
9 8 7 6 5 4 3 2 1

Manufactured in Shenzhen, China HH052018

MIX
Paper from
responsible sources
FSC® C017606
FSC
www.fsc.org

AROUND THE WORLD
IN EVERY VEHICLE

AMBER STEWART

ILLUSTRATED BY
DUNCAN BEEDIE

The Van Go family love their quiet, little corner of the world in Scotland in the United Kingdom.

Every day, Freddie and Daisy cycle up and down their street with friends.

Mom and Dad Van Go fill up their bicycle baskets with food and goods from the local shops, and visit with Grandpa and Grandma.

But there is a **big**, **wide world** out there waiting to be explored.

The little street will still be there for the family when they come home.

They have planned their long summer break, and the Van Go family are heading on a round-the-world trip!

One final check of passports, tickets, and travel money and it's time to pack up their little blue camper van . . .

. . . and start their **big** adventure.

London is their first stop! London is **noisy** and **busy**. Tourists snap pictures in Trafalgar Square.

Black taxicabs drive around and around at Buckingham Palace, looking for fares. They weave between cars and bikes and the big red buses.

The Van Go family take an open-topped bus tour, sitting high up to see the sights.

"What other kinds of buses can you find around the world?" Freddie asks, opening up his journal.

In the morning, the Van Go family arrive in Folkestone, England. They look at the signs.

~PRIDE OF THE SEA~
CHANNEL SEAWAYS

"Are we going to France by ferry?" asks Daisy.
"We're going under the water, not on the water!" says Freddie.
They are taking the car train through the Channel Tunnel to France.

ANGLO-FRANCE AIR

HM COASTGUARD

La Cité

BIENVENUE EN FRANCE!

9834

EUROTUNNEL LE SHUTTLE

The car train is quick. Soon they are driving through the French countryside on their way to Paris. They watch the farmers working the land with tractors, trailers, and combine harvesters.

11

The Parisian streets are a whirl of excitement! Cyclists scoot past them, with baskets full of shopping. Taxis beep and honk along the Champs-Elysées.

Crêpes!

AMBULANCE

TAXI

The Van Go family are going to explore the city by metro.
But Freddie is nervous about going underground.
"Don't worry, Freddie," Mom Van Go says, "many cities have
metro systems. They are a fast and safe way to travel."

All the routes out of Paris are busy, busy, busy!
"I think all the Parisians are going on vacation today,"
sighs Mom.

BEEP!

TOOT! TOOT!

VROOM!

Horns honk, drivers shout, everyone is hot and bothered in the three-lane traffic jam.

14

Slowly the traffic clears and the little blue van rolls through France and into Germany. They follow the River Danube, stopping along the way in pretty villages.

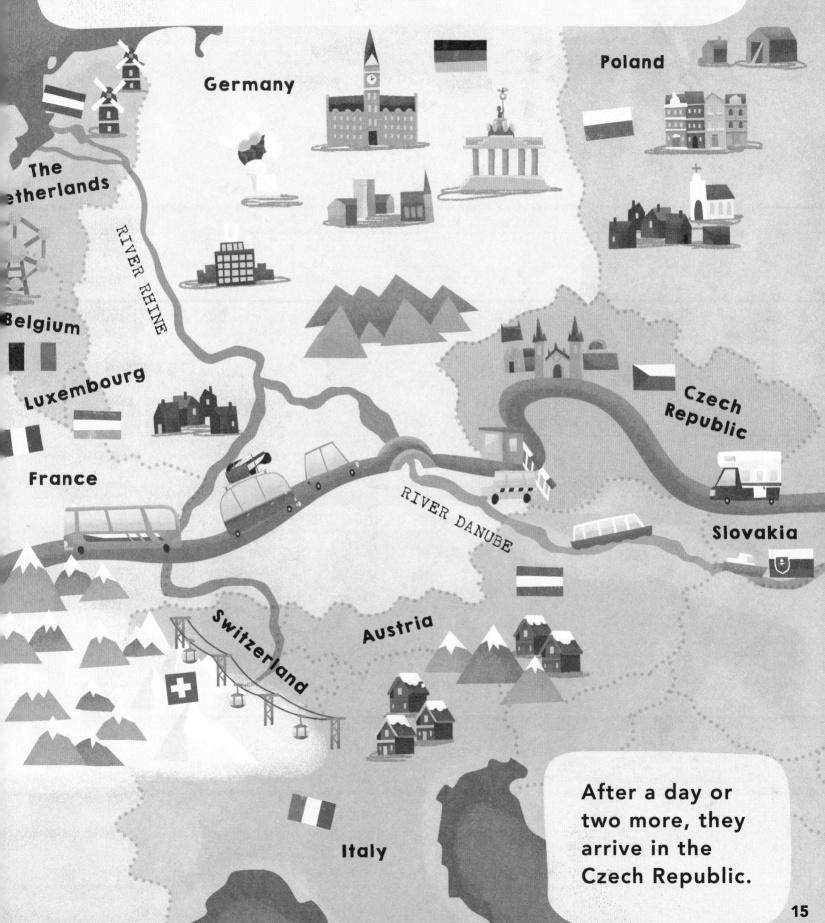

The Netherlands

Germany

Poland

Belgium

RIVER RHINE

Luxembourg

Czech Republic

France

RIVER DANUBE

Slovakia

Switzerland

Austria

Italy

After a day or two more, they arrive in the Czech Republic.

The Van Go family has never seen a city like Prague!

As they walk slowly over Charles Bridge, Daisy and Freddie wave to the people but they don't wave back. "Those are statues, not real people," smiles Mom.

A friendly policeman waves instead, directing traffic this way and that. He shows Daisy and Freddie his police car.

"Police cars look different in other cities but they all help to keep people safe," he says.

NYPD—USA

Keisatsu—JAPAN

Polizia—ITALY

Police—AUSTRALIA

The Van Go family now face quite a test—four days driving across four different countries!

SERBIA to BULGARIA
235 miles

BULGARIA to TURKEY
340 miles

ISTANBUL 63 miles

18

CZECH REP to SLOVAKIA 205 miles

SLOVAKIA to SERBIA 355 miles

Did the little blue van make it? Of course it did: it's the best van in the world!

Istanbul is bustling after dark!

They explore the city by tram.
Voices echo from the decorated
mosques and the streets are full of
laughter and chatter from the cafés.

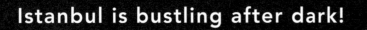

San Francisco—USA

Melbourne—AUSTRALIA

Amsterdam—THE NETHERLANDS
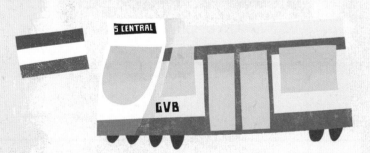

Lisbon—PORTUGAL

"Next trip we can visit other famous cities with trams," says Dad Van Go, as he holds on tight.

Today is a big day for the Van Go gang. Grandpa and Grandma have arrived in Istanbul by airplane.

They will drive the little blue van back home on an adventure of their own.

THE NETHERLANDS

GERMANY

CZECH REPUBL

UNITED KINGDOM

BELGIUM

AUSTR

FRANCE

ITALY

PORTUGAL

SPAIN

TAPAS

Grandpa shows the route they will take on his big fold-out map.

He is looking forward to the food!

The Van Go family are sad to wave goodbye to Grandpa and Grandma but eager to get to the airport to continue their travels.

Freddie and Daisy have never traveled by plane before. Excited, they show their passports . . .

. . . and watch their bags go through Security.

The Van Go family will fly to Mumbai in India, in a huge jumbo jet. At the airport, they see planes of all sizes.

While waiting to take off, Daisy looks up other sorts of planes.

Postal—GERMANY

Passenger—IRELAND

Light aircraft—UNITED KINGDOM

Military—USA

After nearly seven hours in the air, they land smoothly in Mumbai. The Mumbai streets are colorful and noisy. Cars and buses, bicycles piled high, rickshaws, and tuk-tuks all travel this way and that.

They have arrived during the famous food truck festival.
"That one reminds me of our little blue van," points Daisy.

The Van Go family love the food cooked and served from colorful trucks.
"Let's do a food tour one day," laughs Freddie.

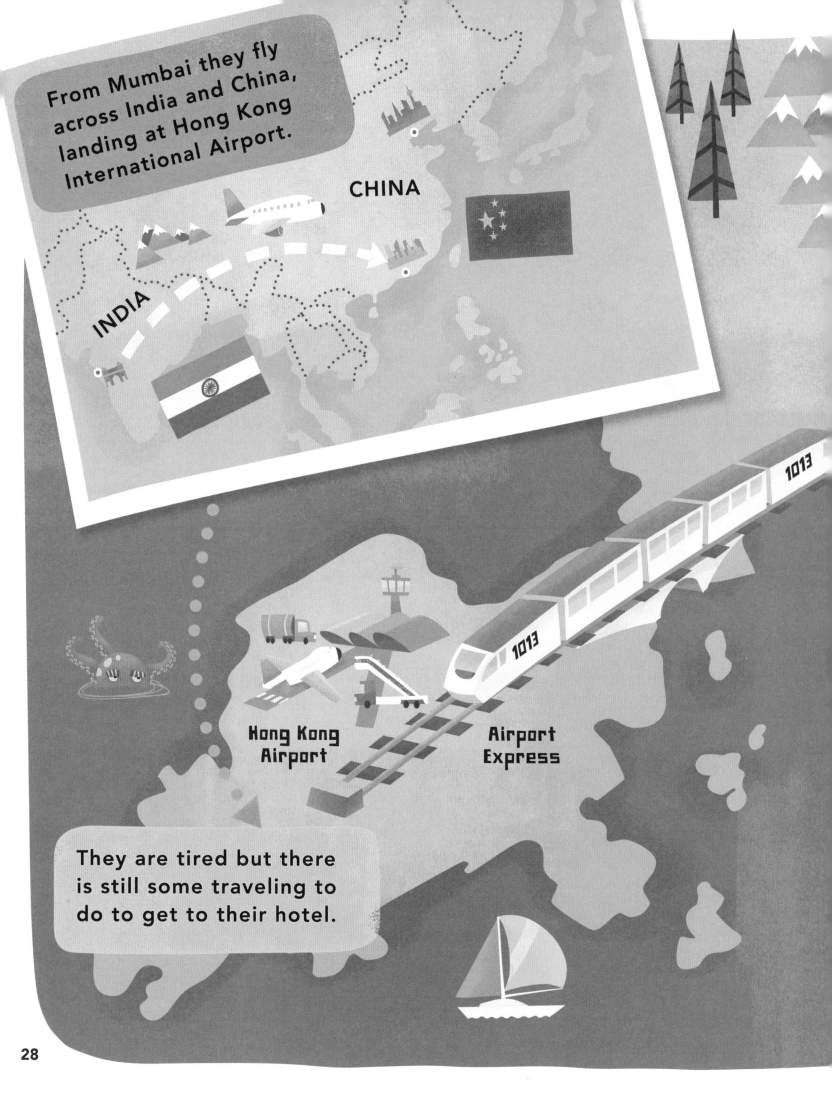

From Mumbai they fly across India and China, landing at Hong Kong International Airport.

CHINA

INDIA

Hong Kong Airport

Airport Express

1013

They are tired but there is still some traveling to do to get to their hotel.

First is the sleek and speedy transit train to the Central Train Station.

"Another train?" yawns Daisy, looking at the bustling station.

Central Train Station

HOTEL

Hotel Transit Bus

Hotel

"No, now a bus!" says Mom Van Go. "A special hotel bus so we don't get lost."

In Hong Kong, they escape the bustle of the modern city and take the Star Ferry in Victoria Harbor.

"Look at all the boats!" shouts Freddie. The harbor is busy with tugboats, fishing boats, and yachts zipping about.

"**Fire! Fire!**" They hear a shout from the harbor. Here comes the maritime fireboat to put out the flames as fire engines race along the shoreline. Soon the fire is out and everyone is safe.

They clap the brave firefighters.

Firefighters are brave all around the world.

FDNY—USA

Wild Fire Plane—AUSTRALIA

LFB—UNITED KINGDOM

SCDF—
SINGAPORE, MALAYSIA

FIRE RESCUE

What a long flight from Hong Kong to their next stop—New York City, the Big Apple!

Mumbai Tuk Tuk ride . . .

EUROTUNNEL 03 09 21

CAR / AUTO

THAMES CABLE CAR ***

314 674 121

ADMIT ONE

Freddie and Daisy fill in a scrapbook diary of their travels so far.

They arrive early in New York, and they find everyone is wide awake and buzzing with activity!

"**Wow!**" says Freddie. "Look at all the yellow cars!"

"They are taxicabs," says Mom Van Go. "Many cities have easy-to-spot taxis. They are the best way to travel if you have a lot of stuff, or if you are in a hurry!"

Tuk-Tuk —THAILAND

Taxi —MEXICO

Black Cab —UNITED KINGDOM

TAXI

Rickshaw—CHINA

US POSTAL

DELIVERY

The family have an amazing time in New York but next stop is Peru.
It's too far for a taxi, of course, so they head back to the airport.

In Peru, Daisy and Freddie are excited to go on an Amazon River
cruise in a steam boat.

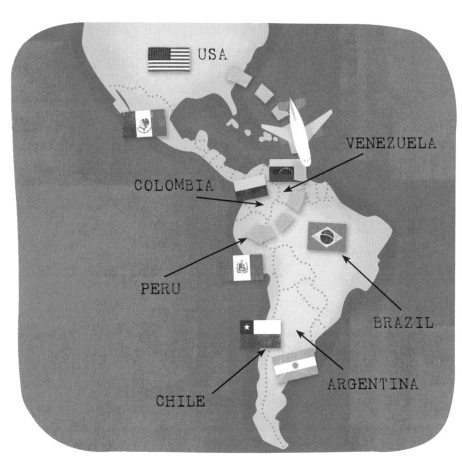

On the way, they spot river dolphins and monkeys.

Next up, Brazil!

The Van Go family has planned a bike tour in Rio de Janeiro. They cycle with their tour guide looking at the water across beaches and lakes.

Whoops! Freddie takes a tumble and grazes his knee.
"I don't think you need an ambulance," smiles Dad, as he
dusts him down. "It's just a little graze. No bones broken."

Freddie would like a ride in an ambulance in any city—he thinks
it would be thrilling to whiz along with the lights flashing.

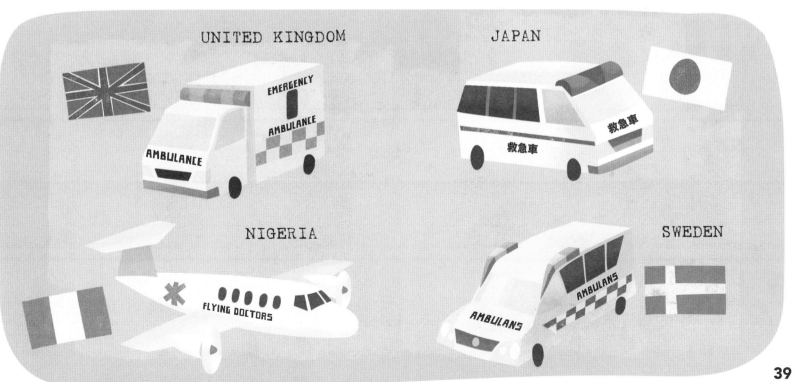

BRAZIL

From Brazil to South Africa, it is a very long journey over the South Atlantic Ocean.

To pass the time, the Van Go family play a game: How long would it take to travel from Rio to Cape Town in different ways?

HOT AIR BALLOON
5 mph = 752 hours

HELICOPTER
250 mph = 15 hours

S.

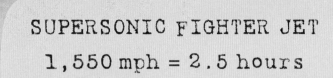

SUPERSONIC FIGHTER JET
1,550 mph = 2.5 hours

306 SP4E

SPACE ROCKET
18,000 mph = 12 mins

JUMBO JET
500 mph = 7.5 hours

FINISH

SOUTH
AFRICA

In Cape Town, there is so much to see and do.

TABLE MOUNTAIN

CAPE VIEW

11

After breakfast in one of the friendly cafés on the Victoria and Alfred waterfront, they take the cable car to the very top of Table Mountain.

While Mom and Dad Van Go admire the view, Freddie looks down at the motorbike riders streaming along the mountain roads.

They are too far away to see the different types of bike but Freddie hopes his favorite—a chopper—is one of them.

Scooter—ITALY

Cruiser—JAPAN

Chopper—USA

Dirt track race bike —GERMANY

The family are sad to leave Cape Town with its beautiful beaches and mountains. The next plane takes them 6,830 miles from Cape Town to Brisbane, Australia.

"Our little blue van!" shout Daisy and Freddie, jumping for joy at the Camper Van Rental Company.

"One just like it," smiles Mom Van Go. "This fits us perfectly." They set off on the five-day Pacific Coast drive from Brisbane to Sydney.

On the way they stop at the Byron Lighthouse . . .

BYRON LIGHTHOUSE

. . . stroke the baby koalas at the Koala Hospital . . .

CAMP

. . . and enjoy the water sports at Palm Beach.

45

Sydney Harbor is the busiest harbor they have ever seen.

The Van Go family look this way and that, from the famous Opera House facing out to sea to the huge ocean liners lit up like Christmas decorations along the harbor walls.

Whoosh! The jet skis zip in and out.

Flap! The sailboats glide around.

AUS 81

AUS 81

The last stop on the amazing world tour is New Zealand. As a special treat, they take a helicopter trip over Milford Sound and see penguins and seals basking in the sun.

It is a very long flight home with changes in several countries.

The Van Go family are happy to return to their little corner of the world, to their family and friends and, of course, their little blue van!

48